KILLER ANIMALS
TIGERS
ON THE HUNT

by Lori Polydoros

Reading Consultant:
Barbara J. Fox
Reading Specialist
North Carolina State University

Content Consultant:
Mahendra Shrestha, PhD
Director, Save The Tiger Fund
National Fish and Wildlife Foundation
Washington, D.C.

Capstone
press

Mankato, Minnesota

Blazers is published by Capstone Press,
151 Good Counsel Drive, P.O. Box 669, Mankato, Minnesota 56002.
www.capstonepress.com

Books published by Capstone Press are manufactured with paper
containing at least 10 percent post-consumer waste.

Library of Congress Cataloging-in-Publication Data
Polydoros, Lori, 1968–
   Tigers : on the hunt / by Lori Polydoros.
   p. cm. — (Blazers. Killer animals)
   Includes bibliographical references and index.
   Summary: "Describes tigers, their physical features, how they hunt and kill, and their role in
the ecosystem" — Provided by publisher.
   ISBN 978-1-4296-3389-5 (library binding)
   1. Tigers — Juvenile literature. I. Title. II. Series.
QL795.T5P65 2010
599.756 — dc22   2009000953

Editorial Credits
Christine Peterson, editor; Kyle Grenz, set designer; Bobbi J. Wyss, book designer;
   Svetlana Zhurkin, media researcher

Photo Credits
Ardea/Chris Brunskill, 10–11
Getty Images/Photographer's Choice/Gary Vestal, 26–27
Minden Pictures/Theo Allofs, 18–19
Peter Arnold/Biosphoto/J.-L. Klein & M.-L. Hubert, 12, 21, 28–29; Pierre Vernay, 4; C. Huetter,
   cover; Wildlife, 7, 17, 24–25
Shutterstock/Anke van Wyk, 8–9; pix2go, 14–15; R. Gino Santa Maria, 22–23

TABLE OF CONTENTS

In the thick grass, a wild boar searches for food. A tiger hides nearby. Its striped **camouflage** coat blends in with the grass. The tiger carefully creeps closer to the boar.

KILLER FACT

Large pads on a tiger's paws allow it to walk quietly.

camouflage – coloring or covering that makes animals blend in with their surroundings

The powerful cat explodes into a **pounce**. It slams the boar to the ground. The tiger sinks its teeth into the boar's neck. The boar dies instantly. The tiger tears into its feast.

KILLER FACT

Each tiger has its own hunting area called a home range.

pounce – to jump on something suddenly

A MIGHTY BUILD

Tigers are the biggest cats in the world. Male tigers weigh as much as 573 pounds (260 kilograms). Females weigh up to 350 pounds (160 kilograms).

KILLER FACT

Each tiger has a different pattern of stripes.

A massive build gives tigers unmatched power. Tigers pin down **prey** with their strong forelegs and huge paws. Razor-sharp claws rip into the flesh of prey.

prey – an animal hunted by another animal

A tiger's sharp teeth work like scissors to cut through **muscle** and break bones. A tiger often kills prey with just one powerful bite to the neck.

KILLER FACT

Tigers may feast on 80 pounds (36 kilograms) of food in one day.

muscle – a part of the body that produces movement

Tigers have **keen** senses. They see in the dark six times better than people. Soft sounds seem very loud to tigers. The crack of a twig might sound like an alarm to tigers!

KILLER FACT

In daylight a tiger's eyesight is about the same as a person's.

keen – able to notice things easily

HUNTING MACHINES

Tigers usually hunt at night. They can **stalk** prey for miles. Tigers crouch behind tall grass and bushes to stay hidden. Their camouflage coats keep prey from seeing them.

stalk – to hunt an animal in a quiet, secret way

A tiger strikes its prey with a quick burst of speed. A tiger's forceful pounce often knocks prey off its feet. The tiger then pins the animal to the ground.

KILLER FACT

Boar and deer are common prey of tigers. But tigers hunt almost any animals including monkeys and porcupines.

Tigers bite the back of the neck to kill small animals. Their bite often breaks the prey's **spinal cord**. Tigers bite the throat of large prey until the animal stops breathing.

KILLER FACT

Tigers drag prey to hiding places before eating. They may drag prey as far as three football fields.

spinal cord – a thick cord of nerve tissue in the neck and back

Tiger Diagram

striped fur

long hind legs

long tail

large paws

muscular shoulders

sharp teeth

strong forelegs

THE FIGHT TO SURVIVE

Tigers help keep the **ecosystem** in balance. They hunt animals that eat plants. Without tigers, these animals would eat too many plants.

ecosystem – a group of animals and plants that work together with their surroundings

Many people hunt tigers even though it is against the law. People also harm tiger **habitats**. These actions kill too many tigers. People must protect these striped stalkers.

habitat – the place and natural conditions in which plants and animals live

Ready to Feast!

GLOSSARY

camouflage (KA-muh-flahzh) — the coloring or covering that makes animals look like their surroundings

ecosystem (EE-koh-sis-tuhm) — a group of animals and plants that work together with their surroundings

habitat (HAB-uh-tat) — the natural place and conditions in which a plant or animal lives

keen (KEEN) — the ability to notice things easily

muscle (MUHSS-uhl) — a part of the body that produces movement; muscles are attached to bones.

pounce (POUNSS) — to jump on something suddenly and grab it

prey (PRAY) — an animal hunted by another animal for food

spinal cord (SPINE-uhl KORD) — a thick cord of nerves that carries signals to the rest of the nerves in the body

stalk (STAWK) — to hunt an animal in a quiet, secret way

READ MORE

Barnes, Julia. *The Secret Lives of Tigers.* The Secret Lives of Animals. Milwaukee: Gareth Stevens, 2007.

Eason, Sarah. *Save the Tiger.* Save The. New York: PowerKids Press, 2009.

Markert, Jenny. *Tigers.* New Naturebooks. Mankato, Minn.: Child's World, 2008.

INTERNET SITES

FactHound offers a safe, fun way to find Internet sites related to this book. All of the sites on FactHound have been researched by our staff.

Here's all you do:

Visit *www.facthound.com*

FactHound will fetch the best sites for you!

INDEX